ils
6112

Lord of the Flies

William Golding

Guide written by Stewart Martin

A Literature Guide for GCSE

Contents

Plot summary

1 *Lord of the Flies* is set on an imaginary, remote tropical island. A plane has crashed while evacuating children from a war-torn country. A group of boys are the only survivors: the members of a church choir and a number of other boys of various ages.

4 Ralph, Jack and Simon (a member of the choir) explore the island and find it uninhabited.

2 Ralph and a fat, short-sighted boy nicknamed Piggy discover a conch shell, and when Ralph blows it all the survivors gather on the beach.

3 Ralph is elected leader of the group, but allows Jack to remain leader of the choir, who are to be hunters. The conch is used to control meetings by giving whoever holds it the right to speak.

14 Jack's tribe hunts Ralph, intending to kill him and, during the hunt, sets fire to the island. A naval officer, whose ship has been attracted by the smoke, rescues them.

12 Ralph's small group tries to keep the signal fire alight. Jack's tribe attacks the group and steals Piggy's glasses to make fire with. Ralph's group goes to demand Piggy's glasses back, taking the conch with them.

13 During the confrontation with Jack's tribe, Piggy is killed and the conch smashed. Ralph escapes, but the rest of his group are captured.

5 Some of the smaller children are frightened by a 'beastie' they think they have seen in the jungle at night, but the older boys dismiss this idea.

7 A ship's smoke is seen on the horizon, but the signal fire has gone out because the choir is hunting. The ship passes. The hunters return with a killed pig and there is a tense confrontation between the two groups about the fire being out.

6 Ralph says they need shelters on the beach and a signal fire on the mountain. Jack volunteers the hunters to keep the fire burning. Jack learns to hunt the pigs on the island, while Ralph and a few others build a few rickety shelters.

8 At night a dead pilot parachutes onto the mountain after a battle high above the island. When the dead pilot is discovered, terror spreads among the boys, who think it is 'the beast'.

11 Jack's tribe holds a great feast and performs a ritual dance, during which Simon returns. He is attacked and killed as 'the beast' by the dancing, chanting boys.

10 Simon falls into a fit, in which he has a 'conversation' with the dead pig's head, then faints. When he recovers, Simon climbs the mountain alone and sees 'the beast' for what it is.

9 Following an unsuccessful challenge for the leadership, Jack sets up his own 'tribe', which hunts and kills a pig and leaves its head as an offering for the beast.

Who's who in *Lord of the Flies*

Ralph

Ralph's character develops as the novel progresses. Unlike Jack, he becomes more aware of the <u>inner nature</u> of humankind. He is, at the beginning, a happy yet <u>sensitive</u> and <u>responsible</u> person who eventually comes to understand the 'darkness of man's heart'. He demonstrates <u>courage, authority, compassion</u> and <u>respect</u> for civilised values. These moral standards are crushed in a world which is run by Jack's kind of rules. Ralph's <u>failure</u> to lead a democratic society successfully symbolises the failure of humankind to recognise or deal with the force of <u>evil</u> within itself.

Piggy

Piggy's physical appearance, his <u>common sense</u> and <u>scientific, intellectual</u> point of view make him the only <u>adult-type</u> figure on the island. He continually shatters the boys' illusions and interrupts their desire to play. When the 'play' develops into something much more sinister, he is killed because he spoils 'the game'. By then, the game has become a terrible reality, a war between good and evil.

Jack

Jack is a leader, but his methods are the natural <u>opposite</u> to those of Ralph. Jack is <u>dictatorial</u> and <u>aggressive</u>; he has a strong desire to lead and asserts himself through his prowess as a <u>hunter</u>, which deteriorates into lust for killing. The character of Jack shows how, without the

6

restrictions of adults or society, certain people revert to primitive desires and actions. Jack's character degenerates as the story unfolds. At the start he asserts his superiority through his background, but he is irresponsible and needs his rewards straight away. He has no patience with constructive, positive things, which is why he grows tired of debates and hut building. His love of hunting stems from the sense of power killing gives him. He abuses his power as a leader, and his freedom from social restraints unleashes the evil latent within his character.

Roger

Roger does not so much develop as a character as reveal his nature through the course of the book. He represents the merciless type of killer and torturer whose sadistic tendencies are let loose on society if dictators take control. Characters like Roger are not leaders, but help to make tyrannical leaders stronger.

Simon

Simon represents the mystic; he has vision and intuition and is the saint or Christ-like figure who has compassion for his fellows. Often, mystics enter 'trances' to find the truth they are seeking. Simon is subject to fainting and hallucinations and his fits symbolise the visionary experience. His conversation with the Lord of the Flies (the dead pig's head) crystallises Golding's message, which is that evil is within everyone, and each individual must wrestle with 'the beast' within. Simon's response is to continue with his quest for truth. He is rejected as 'batty' and slaughtered in a ritual frenzy. He represents the martyr who is neither valued nor understood by his society.

About the author

William Golding

William Golding was born in the village of St. Columb Minor in Cornwall in 1911. His father was a schoolmaster and his mother a suffragette. Both his parents had radical and progressive ideas and encouraged him to study science both at Marlborough and later at Brasenose College, Oxford.

However, Golding had always been interested in literature and had begun writing at the age of seven. After two years of studying science at Oxford he read English Literature instead, becoming a keen scholar of Anglo-Saxon. His first book, a volume of poems, was published in 1935, the year before he graduated from Oxford.

After graduating, Golding worked for a time as a settlement house worker and in 1939 he moved to Salisbury where he taught English at the Bishop Wordsworth's School. In 1940 he joined the Royal Navy in which he served for six years. He spent most of this time at sea on active service, and was involved in a number of naval actions including the sinking of the German battleship Bismark and the invasion of Normandy in 1944.

When the war was over, Golding returned to teaching and writing but his experiences in the war had had a profound effect on his view of life. He no longer believed in the innocence of human beings and his view of humanity had been darkened by his experiences. He had come to believe that without the laws and social pressures that keep order in society, a dark and ruthless side of human nature emerges.

It was against this background that *Lord of the Flies* was published in 1954. This was followed by *The Inheritors* in 1955 which describes the wiping out of Neanderthal man by Homo Sapiens. *Pincher Martin*, published in 1956, is the story of a naval officer who faces a struggle for survival after his ship is torpedoed. Golding's next novel, *Free Fall* (1959) is about the artist, Sammy Mountjoy, who reflects on his past life and his loss of freedom.

Golding left teaching in 1961 in order to give all his time to writing. His next novel, *The Spire,* published in 1964, is the story of the building of a cathedral spire. The building project sparks off various problems which result in treachery and murder. He went on to write a number of other novels, a play called *The Brass Butterfly* (1958), three short novels under the title *The Scorpion God* (1971) and various essays and autobiographical pieces.

In 1980 he won the Booker Prize for his novel *Rites of Passage*, the first volume of a trilogy which continued with *Close Quarters* (1987) and, his last published novel, *Fire Down Below* (1989). In 1983 he was awarded the Nobel Prize for Literature. He died in Perranarworthal, Cornwall, in 1993.

Historical background

Golding's first novel, *Lord of the Flies* deals with one of the themes that was to recur throughout his work – that of the conflict between barbarism and civilisation. It focuses on the idea that when the trappings of social restraints and civilising influences are stripped away and life becomes a battle for survival then the innate cruelty and barbarism within human beings emerges.

This view of life was, no doubt, shaped by his wartime experiences. He had been appalled by the brutalities committed by the Germans and the Japanese, and these events gave him cause to rethink his ideas on the nature of evil and to explore and understand how people who are supposed to be 'civilised' can commit 'evil' acts. His experience as a teacher also allowed him to observe the behaviour of young boys in group situations. In many ways, *Lord of the Flies* is part of this exploration. The novel seems to conclude that for the vast majority of individuals it is only laws, social pressure and the threat of punishment which prevent people behaving in an evil way.

Golding based his idea on a popular children's novel of the nineteenth century, *Coral Island* by R.M.Ballantyne. In this novel three British schoolboys, Ralph, Jack and Peterkin are shipwrecked on an island. They face many problems, including encounters with pirates, wild animals and cannibals, but they all work together and keep their British 'civilised' standards in the face of all these 'uncivilised' adversaries.

Golding moves his story into modern times – his group of children are being evacuated by plane because a nuclear war has broken out. When this plane crashes, all the adults are killed and the boys have to pick their own leaders and establish their own rules. However, the democratic ideas that they initially establish soon break down, the strongest (and most brutal) dominate the rest and tyranny reigns. The weaker members of the group become the target of, to begin with, teasing or torment, and later vicious persecution ending in death for some of the boys.

This is Golding's pessimistic, but perhaps realistic, view of human nature. Although the boys have been taught the rules and social standards of civilised behaviour, when these are removed or break down savagery and evil dominate. In his collected essays, *The Hot Gates*, there is a piece about his first novel, *Lord of the Flies*, called 'Fable', in which he says, 'Before the Second World War I believed in the perfectibility of social man; that a correct structure of society would produce goodwill; and that therefore you could remove all social ills by a reorganisation of society. It is possible that today I believe something of the same again; but after the war I did not because I was unable to. I had discovered what one man could do to another.'

Lord of the Flies offers a disturbing insight into real human nature.

Themes and images

Fear and the beast

The beast represents the way in which people make something outside of themselves evil, so that they can maintain an image of themselves as good. This allows them to avoid the responsibility of looking carefully inside themselves – it allows them to avoid self-knowledge.

Golding uses the boys' imagination, daydreams and nightmares to show us their fears and desires. These things illuminate the sense of loss in the children, and their need for security. The snakes are only present on the island in the boys' imaginations. The snake image is traditionally symbolic of evil and is appropriate for Golding's argument that evil comes from within. The beast gives the boys' fear something to focus on. There are several kinds of fear depicted in the novel, apart from the obvious physical fear of the trapped piglet at the start and (in a different sense) the trapped Ralph at the end. Fear is often, although not always, associated with guilt. There is the fear of the truth, as when the boys do not at first want to accept that they may never be rescued. Later, some of them do not want to accept that they killed Simon. There is the spiritual fear of the beast that is themselves, which is why they will not listen to Simon.

The arrival of the dead parachutist gives a physical form to the beast. In reality he is a pathetic figure, killed in war and robbed of all human dignity in death. The moving, decomposing corpse is macabre, but there is nothing supernatural about it. It takes its place in nature, along with the flies that feast on it, and is finally claimed by the sea.

Defects exist in any human society and they are usually caused by defects in human nature – what Golding sees as the constant but undeveloped evil resident within all humankind. This is the beast. What happens in the novel is an example of how, in the right set of circumstances, the beast will reveal itself and bring about corruption.

Civilisation and order

The conch is a beautiful object, a part of the natural world which is untouched and unspoilt by people. It becomes a symbol of authority, common sense and democratic discipline. Its destruction symbolises the wilful destruction of order and rational behaviour.

In Greek mythology, the conch was used by the sea god Triton to calm or raise the oceans. Notice as you read the novel which characters respect the conch, which ones simply obey it and which ones challenge and finally disregard its authority. The boys gradually lose their innocence in the novel – echoed in the way the conch loses its colour.

The concern of some of the boys with rules and order echoes a basic requirement for civilisation. Civilisation is culture which has advanced beyond the primitive and savage. At first the boys are products of civilised culture; at the end they are degenerate remnants of a small, isolated group, which has stripped itself of the refinements of moral values.

The assembly is the boys' attempt at a democratically organised form of government. It begins well, but the presence of two natural leaders causes a split in the power structure of the boys' society and leads to its break-up. The conch is the assembly's symbol of authority. The attempt to organise a democratic society, where each member has a voice, fails when Jack's regime emerges as a dictatorship. Responsibility is a quality necessary for good leadership in a civilised society. It is displayed by Ralph, but discarded by Jack.

Nature

Golding sets his novel on an unspoiled island, which effectively isolates his characters from the world. He creates a microcosm (a mini-world), and by making us look closely at the nature of this microcosm he makes us consider the real, 'whole' world and the condition of humankind.

The sea represents the vast distance between the boys and the civilisation from which they are cut off. The contrast between the sea on one side of the island and the sea on the other side, echoes the division between the two groups of boys. Similarly, the storm creates a background to the increasing tension and exploding violence in the boys' experience. Showing nature in sympathy with the moods and feelings of man is a common device in literature. It is sometimes known as 'pathetic fallacy', which is the crediting of nature or inanimate objects with human emotions.

Golding's descriptions of the vegetation and natural life on the island work on two levels: they reinforce mood and reflect the continuing beauty in nature. Nature is shown as balanced and unified, in contrast with the divisions appearing among the boys. For example, food is a natural resource of the island but has painful repercussions: fruit gives the boys diarrhoea and pig meat comes to symbolise power. Interestingly, the boys make little use of the sea as a source of food.

Images of heat are also frequent. Heat is the first force to change the boys' usual behaviour. It appears in two different forms: natural heat, like the temperature of the island, and the heat of fire. Both forms are often used to emphasise the emotional, 'primeval' heat in certain characters.

Power

The desire for power and its relationship to leadership is a major area of conflict in the boys' situation. Both Jack and Ralph are 'leader-types'. The conflict arises because of their differing methods and morals. From the first time we see Jack in the novel it is clear that he already has power, as he is leader of the choir. His way of ordering the boys to do as he says gives us an early glimpse of the way he uses and exhibits his power over others. When Ralph is democratically elected as leader, it is obvious that Jack is furious. Ralph is sensitive to this and so appeases him by giving him command of the choir, who will become the 'hunters'. However, Jack is not content with this limited power for very long and soon a power struggle develops between him and Ralph. Eventually, Ralph is inevitably the loser in this struggle because he still clings to the civilised values of reason and fair play, whereas Jack uses the ruthless tactics of the dictator. When the title 'chief' is adopted by Jack it indicates a change in emphasis from the leadership of Ralph. The trappings of being chief include position and respect – like they did for Ralph – but Jack's style of leadership also commands fear and obedience. Physique plays an important part in the way the boys see themselves and their credibility within the group. Notice that the two leaders are the biggest, strongest boys on the island.

Piggy's glasses symbolise reason, the ability to see clearly, and man's inhumanity to man (as when they are broken and then stolen). Throughout the novel the fate of the glasses illustrates the loss of reasonable behaviour. The breaking of the glasses coincides with the abandonment of civilised values. The glasses also come to symbolise power. They have the power to create fire and so whoever possesses the glasses has the power to control this fundamental element to survival on the island. This is one of the underlying reasons why Jack wants them and why, when he gets them, he wears them at his waist as a symbol of his power and authority.

Savagery

Play and 'fun' result from the boys' pleasure in having their own island. It is a daytime escape from night-time fears for the littluns. For the older boys, play is distorted into a sinister, devilish activity. Fun develops into irresponsibility, then into torture and murder. Notice, for example, how 'trundling' rocks provides an innocent pastime at first, but in the end, rocks are deadly weapons.

One of the movements traceable through the novel is in the choir, who change to hunters, to a tribe, to savages. This downward path is sometimes known as atavism. Each experience of killing changes the boys and widens the gap between the hunters and those who cling to civilised values. The boys eventually descend to a primitive level of savagery ruled by an arrogant chief. At this stage they are no longer recognisable, physically or mentally, as the boys described at the start of the novel. Golding leaves us to imagine what kind of adults they might become after their experiences on the island. The first clear sign of the emergence of the savage is the mask. At first the mask is intended as camouflage, but it generates a strange and primitive freedom in the wearer. The mask contributes to the degeneration of the tribe. 'Tribe' is the word used by Jack to describe his band of followers. At first the word suggests an element of play, but the tribe quickly develops into a savage band of killers.

Rituals offer security and reassurance and are used by societies to make events feel more important and permanent, whether these are the rituals of joining a gang, of a marriage service, or those of the church. Ritual emerges as a powerful force on the island. Through rituals of chant, dance and superstition, the tribe is held together and commits atrocities. The chant of the hunters is a ritual which is repeated, growing in fierceness on each occasion. The most extreme violence of the chant coincides with the breaking of the last barriers of civilised behaviour, when Simon is murdered.

One way of looking at this novel is to consider it as being structured around six hunts. Each successful hunt brings the boys closer to the savage side of human nature. The pig is the object of the hunt, as a source of food. But the pig-hunt becomes a symbol of the decline of civilised values and the loss of innocence. As 'Lord of the Flies', the sow's head illustrates the superstitious, ritualistic level to which the tribe of hunters has sunk.

Darkness and death

Darkness in the novel is both a time of fear and a symbol of evil and degradation. The darkness can be literal, as with the darkness of the jungle and of night, and in this form it starts off as harmless and natural. Darkness becomes more spiritual with the mention of the beast. From this point on, the natural darkness of night gradually becomes the superstitious 'darkness' of ignorance and fear. Eventually it becomes 'the darkness of man's heart'.

Light symbolises freedom from ignorance. The riotous colours and fierce light of day are contrasted with the loss of security that darkness brings.

There are three human deaths on the island that we know about for certain. The first is of a littlun, by accident; the second is of Simon, by crazed excitement; and the third is of Piggy, by savage murder. These deaths, and the different reasons for them, symbolise the boys' degeneration. The deaths of the pigs chart the hunters' movement towards total savagery. Initially, the hunters are unable to kill a piglet. You should also consider death in the novel within the context of the atomic bomb and the dead pilot who drops onto the island.

Text commentary

Chapters 1–4

Chapter 1

> **The boy with the fair hair lowered himself down the last few feet of rock...**

Piggy is <u>physically</u> <u>disadvantaged</u>: he is short, fat, very short-sighted, and suffers from asthma. He can't run and he can't swim. Look out for evidence of this.

Ralph, in contrast, is tall, fair, agile, a good swimmer with a 'mildness about his mouth and eyes that proclaimed no devil'. Golding saw him as 'the average, rather more than average, man of goodwill and common sense; the man who makes mistakes because he simply does not understand at first the nature of the disease from which they all suffer'.

Notice that it is the <u>heat</u> which is the first force to create a change in the boys' usual behaviour. Notice also how the fruit gives the boys diarrhoea. This is the first hint that their Garden of Eden may not be as perfect as it at first seems.

> **'I don't care what they call me ... so long as they don't call me what they used to call me at school.'**

Piggy doesn't care what they call him – so long as it isn't 'Piggy'. The nickname 'Piggy' firmly establishes the way his peers see him – his 'type'. Notice the irony that, in the novel itself, the pig is first of all a beast, then a ritual offering to the beast, then Lord of the Flies; at the same time the name 'Piggy' is used for the most <u>rational</u> <u>person</u> in the group.

Piggy is the character in the novel about whom we change our minds the most, although he himself does not change at all. One of Piggy's characteristics is his consistency, as shown in his friendship (for Ralph).

Explore

Piggy does not seem to change his mind much. Why do you think this is so?

It is ironic that Piggy possesses so many of the qualities needed for a leader in this situation (logic, reason, understanding of organisation and the group), yet is totally unsuitable for the role of Chief because of other qualities of character and background. See how far these contradictions are revealed at the outset and consider what Piggy's actual role is (or should be) on the island.

> *Ralph did a surface dive and swam under water with his eyes open.*

Explore

Does Golding do this with any other character? (Look at Chapter 9.)

At the start, Ralph is a <u>fun-loving</u> boy, excited by the prospect of adventure without the restrictions of grown-up authority. We see many events through his eyes and are given many insights into the way he feels about events and people.

Piggy is a <u>realist</u>. He explains that they need to face the fact that no one knows their location, and that they must <u>organise</u> <u>themselves</u>. Compare this reaction with Ralph's early pleasure at being on a beautiful island. In many ways, Ralph is a typical product of the British middle class. His father is a naval commander and Ralph apparently has a <u>happy</u> <u>family</u> <u>background</u>. However, his dream in Chapter 7 suggests that his mother is dead or his parents are divorced and he sees less than he would like of his father. He represents the model son, a good boy with a sense of the importance of <u>democracy</u>, but at the same time <u>fun-loving</u> <u>and</u> <u>easy-going</u>.

> **_In colour the shell was deep cream, touched here and there with fading pink._**

Piggy has acquired valuable knowledge and information during his life. He recognises the <u>value</u> of the conch. Although Ralph finds the conch in the lagoon and is attracted by its <u>beauty</u>, it is Piggy who advises of its practical use to make a loud noise which will attract other survivors. The first time the conch is blown, it heralds the birth of civilised order on the island. Contrast this with what happens when the conch is blown for the last time. Why do you think Ralph does not blow the conch when he calls the meeting in Chapter 4?

Explore

The conch is blown seven times in *Lord of the Flies*. Look at each one in turn. When does blowing the conch lead to stirring things up, and when does it lead to quietening them down?

> **_he shouted an order and they halted_**

Jack collects the choir around him. They wear a black uniform. The <u>military</u> <u>discipline</u> of the choir is more striking than its religious character. This is ominous. Some critics have seen Jack as a representation of Hitler, and the choir as an image for the Nazis. It is possible that Golding had this in his mind, but he could just as easily have had in mind the type of people who have become powerful forces in society in the past, and who continue to do so. Such people usually begin as dedicated revolutionaries, and form tight-knit groups under strong leadership. But they often impose their values upon others by means of force and become <u>corrupt</u> <u>and</u> <u>vicious</u> <u>tyrants</u>.

Explore

Which words and phrases suggest Jack's authority, determination and power?

Even though he has been in a catastrophic air crash, and is now on an island very different from the one he left, Jack carries on as leader of the choir and treats the choristers strictly. At Jack's first appearance in the novel, we recognise him as a <u>natural</u> <u>leader</u>.

Jack wears the uniform of the head chorister. Later, he and his choristers change to another kind of 'uniform' – one of painted faces and masks. Notice the colour of the choristers' cloaks. Black and red are traditionally associated with evil, magic, the devil and hell-fire, and are connected with Jack throughout the novel. The colours he later paints on the mask are red, white and black, and he has red hair. At one level, Jack's red hair suggests a short and <u>fiery</u> <u>temper</u>. At another level, Jack's connections with the colour red suggest blood, or hell and the devil. Contrast these suggestions with Golding's description of Ralph's appearance – especially his eyes. What does this tell us about the kind of leader Jack is? Jack does not want to be known by his first name. What does this tell you about his character? What is Jack called by the end of the book?

Text commentary

> **'He's not Fatty,' cried Ralph, 'his real name's Piggy.'**

Piggy needs to be accepted by the others, but is <u>vulnerable</u> to their <u>mockery</u>. Notice his reaction to their teasing about his nickname. How does Ralph react? What can you learn of Ralph's character from this?

When the laughter dies away we meet Roger, a 'slight, furtive boy'. At this stage his character is unrevealed and he is something of a mystery.

Explore

Would you agree that those personal characteristics which caused Ralph to be elected as leader are the same ones which make his leadership ineffective as the story progresses?

Jack feels he has a natural right to be the leader. Golding says he has <u>'arrogance'</u>. Why do you think Ralph feels the need to compromise, to 'offer something'? <u>Decision-making</u> is an important part of government. Notice Ralph's need to have time to think – he says 'I can't decide what to do straight off.' Do you think this weakens Ralph's leadership?

Simon is described as a 'skinny, vivid little boy', who is prone to fainting. Is there any hint in Chapter 1 that he sees things differently from the other boys?

Because of his physique, Piggy is made an 'outsider', and is excluded from the group of explorers. Can you think why he should, by rights, have been included?

> **"Ralph shaded his eyes and followed the jagged outline of the crags up towards the mountain."**

A major feature of the island is the mountain. Many mountains feature significantly in the Bible (for example, when Moses receives the Law of God and the Ten Commandments), and in many parts of the world mountains are holy places. Typically, mountains have to be climbed to find the truth. At first the boys climb the mountain to discover the truth of their whereabouts. Later, Simon climbs the mountain to find out the truth about the beast: it is only a dead man.

The island is described as 'roughly boat-shaped'. Interestingly, the boys never seriously consider building a boat to escape – they wait for a boat to come to them.

Explore

Why might Golding have wanted to keep the boys on the island?

The boys find buds on some bushes. How do their different reactions illustrate the differences in their characters? Notice how Simon says they are 'like candles'. Think about what Simon represents in the novel, and why his naming of the buds is appropriate. (Where would you expect to see candles burning? What do the candles represent?)

> **❝I was just waiting for a moment to decide where to stab him.❞**

Jack is seen here as still being a product of civilisation. He is unable to kill 'because of the enormity of the knife descending... the unbearable blood.' Notice the change in Jack after his first successful hunt.

Chapter 2

> **❝There aren't any grown-ups.❞**

Ralph's natural inclination is towards orderly and <u>democratic</u> assemblies. Notice how the conch is to be used as the visible symbol of authority and to show who has the right to speak. How does Golding convey the idea that Jack's notion of fun includes <u>bullying, punishment</u> and <u>violence</u>? Can you find more evidence of this later in the novel?

> **❝It's like in a book.❞**

The references to children's books illustrate the <u>adventure and excitement</u> which are offered to children through imaginative fiction. The boys' experience on the island does not parallel stories in these <u>unrealistic</u> books.

Many writers from the early twentieth century tended to promote values and virtues which were considered to be characteristically 'British'. After the Second World War, Golding and others showed the fragility of such virtues, and revealed how easily <u>savagery</u> can take over from order. After all, in 'normal' life, none of the boys represented order more than Jack Merridew.

Explore

Do you think that the novel's moral is 'terrible' and that Golding's view of people is 'inhuman'? Or do you think that he has a realistic view of what human beings are capable of?

Golding did not want to make his novel too realistic because 'People do not much like moral lessons. The pill has to be sugared, has to be witty or entertaining, or engaging in some way or another.' Talking about *Lord of the Flies*, he said: 'If the pill is not sufficiently sugared it will not be swallowed. If the moral is terrible enough he [the author] will be regarded as inhuman; and if the edge of his parable cuts deeply enough, he will be crucified.'

> **"Until the grown-ups come to fetch us we'll have fun."**

Ralph is in no doubt that grown-ups will rescue them. He thinks the boys can have fun while they are waiting. In contrast, Piggy shows that he has a sense of priorities. He is not afraid to speak out, even when what he has to say is unpopular. Ralph tells the assembly that he thinks there are two important things in life on the island – fun and rescue.

> **"Tell us about the snake-thing."**

One of the littluns says that he is afraid of a 'beastie'. The word 'beast' is used in many ways in the novel. On this occasion, what the littlun calls 'a snake thing' is simply an optical illusion created by the creepers. Here, 'the beast' could simply be a small child's nightmare. Can you think of deeper meanings? (Think of what it was that destroyed innocence in the Garden of Eden.)

Traditionally fire symbolises power and hope as well as fear and destruction. Fire brings warmth, comfort and a sense of safety, but equally can destroy everything in its path. You can think about the ways in which Golding uses all the different meanings attached to fire in this novel. A similar sort of ambiguity surrounds the hunters: obtaining food necessary for survival versus destroying the community by wanton killing.

Piggy hates <u>irresponsible</u> behaviour. Why do you think he criticises the boys for behaving 'like a crowd of kids', when that is exactly what they are? He is helpless and terrified when Jack takes his glasses to make a fire, in case he doesn't return them. Piggy is completely dependent upon his glasses, and therefore on the goodwill of those who borrow them.

Explore

Carefully read Jack's speech: 'I agree... do the right things.' Compare his beliefs here with his behaviour later in the novel.

Jack denies Piggy the right to speak. In contrast, Ralph supports Piggy's claim to speak because he has the conch. Is Jack showing signs of wishing to be a dictator? Does Ralph believe in democracy? Does Jack say one thing then do another? Does Jack's character worsen as the novel progresses, or was he in fact not very noble to begin with?

> *The flames, as though they were a kind of wild life, crept as a jaguar creeps on it belly*

At first the flame of the fire is 'a squirrel', leaping from tree to tree, but as the fire grows, so the image becomes a <u>fiercer</u> animal that 'gnaws'. Then the image becomes a jaguar, a predator which 'creeps on its belly' towards its prey. Can you see how Golding draws a parallel with the destructive passion developing among the boys?

Notice how the language hints at future events: Piggy glances 'into hell' and later, 'the crowd' (not 'the boys') stand 'silent as death'.

> *How can you expect to be rescued if you don't put first things first and act proper?*

How does Ralph respond to Piggy's <u>accusations</u> of carelessness above? Notice how Jack repeats the words a short while later. How does Jack react to accurate, reasonable criticism? What do you learn about Jack from this? Do you agree that Piggy's weakness is that although there is often good sense in what he says, he seems unable to convince the group of anything? Ralph is the only one who listens to Piggy's ideas. Which other character does nobody listen to?

Piggy represents the power of 'conscience'. He frequently cautions the others to consider what grown-ups would think of their behaviour. Why is it not surprising that Piggy is the one to notice that a littlun is missing? Why do you think Piggy is so 'adult' for his age? (Consider his upbringing, and how his isolation from 'normal' boyish behaviour because of his physique and ill-health might have affected his character.) What do you think of Piggy from the first two chapters? Would life have been different on the island if Piggy had been voted chief? Notice how Ralph's attitude towards Piggy has changed by the end of the book.

Explore

How does your attitude to Piggy change from the start to the end of the novel? Try to pinpoint exactly when Ralph changes his mind about Piggy.
(Look towards the end of Chapter 4.)

❝The crowd was as silent as death❞

The first death is of the littlun with the birthmark. Later, Simon and Piggy die, and they too have physical 'defects'. Do any of the other boys have physical defects like these three? Is it true that only the boys with physical defects get killed? Why does Golding make this happen? Were the three boys vulnerable simply because they were not physically perfect? Or is this Golding's way of hinting that these characters are special, and that we are to think more deeply about exactly what makes them outsiders?

❝A tree exploded in the fire❞

The Bible story of the Garden of Eden presents the snake as evil. Snake images are used in this way throughout the novel. The burning creepers look like snakes and as such are something to fear. The last sentence of this chapter contains powerful symbolism. Traditionally, when might you hear a drum roll? Is this side of the island really 'unfriendly'? The description at the beginning of Chapter 7 explains why the boys might feel this way.

Chapter 3

❝The silence of the forest❞

While practising hunting techniques, Jack is startled by 'a harsh cry that seemed to come out of the abyss of ages'. This underlines the gap that exists between modern civilisation and past ages, when primitive man had to hunt in order to survive.

Explore

List the words and phrases that describe Jack's body movements changing from those of a civilised boy into those of a hunter.

When he returns, Jack tries to talk about the primitive feeling for the hunt which is growing inside him. Outwardly, there is 'madness' in his eyes.

❝They're batty.❞

Jack's growth into the leading savage contrasts with the other boys' attempts to maintain a civilised society on the beach. Ralph gives two reasons for building huts. What are they? The collapse of a hut means a heavier workload for Ralph, but what does it represent in terms of civilisation on the island? Why are the boys so reluctant to build huts?

Jack, Ralph and Simon have been discussing the littluns' nightmares and their intense fear at night. Jack admits to sensing something fearful when he is alone in the jungle. To what does he compare this feeling? What is Golding telling us here about the dark side of the human mind? (Re-read the section 'The beast' on pages 13–14 for help with these questions.)

Manual work has no appeal for Piggy. He does not help Ralph build the huts. Can you connect this with Piggy's belief that 'life is scientific'? Notice the widening gap between Jack and Ralph.

> **❝his eyes so bright they had deceived Ralph into thinking him delightfully gay and wicked❞**

Simon's bright eyes suggest to Ralph that he is both 'delightfully gay' (meaning happy and carefree) and 'wicked'. What do you think the brightness of Simon's eyes illustrates? Events and images surrounding Simon often parallel Bible stories of Christ. Simon helps his fellow humans, struggles with 'the devil', and is finally killed by people who fail to understand him. Golding uses pearl and opal as colour images in connection with Simon. Why do you think he chooses these luminous colours?

Explore

Read the description of the acres of fruit trees. Golding describes the world of nature as the Garden of Eden. Given this religious reference, what is Golding suggesting in the rest of this chapter?

Read the description of Simon finding his den in the foliage. The butterfly motif recurs the next time Simon visits his den. What do you think the butterflies symbolise? Think about their delicacy and their fragile, short-lived beauty.

Golding's beautiful description of the foliage as night falls serves to portray Simon at one with the natural world. Why is this appropriate? Both Jack and Simon go into the jungle alone – but Jack is pleased when other boys join him, whereas Simon wants to make sure that nobody follows him.

Chapter 4

> **❝Strange things happened at midday.❞**

The lagoon is both a symbol of safety and a place of illusions. Notice how this contrasts with the sea on the other side of the island. What effect does the simile 'the sun gazed down like an angry eye' have? The intense midday light creates optical illusions. How do the boys react to these illusions? Piggy's approach is typically scientific.

Note how civilised time – represented by watches – has been replaced by nature's time, and nature's 'rhythms'. Piggy wants to build a sundial. Read on in this chapter and try to discover why he should want to do this.

> *Percival was mouse-coloured and had not been very attractive even to his mother.*

Percival is a pathetic character. What does he represent in terms of what the children have lost? Golding describes the 'corporate life' of the littluns. Their 'generic title' (a group name rather than personal names) reinforces our sense of their <u>dwindling individuality</u>. Younger than the others, they have had less time to learn the ways of society. They seem to be <u>losing</u> the refinements of civilisation. Do you consider the older boys neglectful of the littluns? Is it their fault that the littluns suffer from eating too much unripe fruit?

Sand castles are being built by the littluns – symbolic of a child's <u>sense</u> <u>of</u> <u>romance</u> <u>and</u> <u>adventure</u>. This description neatly conjures up the atmosphere of very small children at play. What changes do the sunshine and daylight bring? How would you describe the way the littluns feel? Are they really happy?

> *Roger gathered a handful of stones and began to throw them.*

How does Roger reveal some indication of his hidden, sadistic tendencies? Do you find Roger's actions surprising? Golding wrote: 'I have lived for many years with small boys, and understand and know them with awful precision.' Looking at Roger as one example, do you think that Golding is right?

Roger's behaviour is only tempered by his upbringing in the civilised world. What is Golding saying about the character of humankind?

What is Golding indicating in his description of Henry controlling the creatures at the sea's edge? Notice Henry's absorption in play and how he treats the little animals. Look at the way Roger behaves towards Henry.

Jack brings coloured clay to paint his face. What reason does he have for doing this? Do you think that at this point Jack understands the power of a <u>mask</u>?

How does the mask widen the gap between Ralph and Jack? Ask yourself what Jack is becoming and to what Ralph is clinging. A <u>painted</u> <u>mask</u> offers an external picture of what is happening within Jack – he is regressing to a <u>primitive</u> <u>form</u>. Jack sees his reflection as an 'awesome stranger'. Why do you think he is so delighted with this? From what does the mask release him?

Notice how personal appearance is important to Jack in his <u>lust for power</u>. Contrast this with Ralph's worries about his increasingly dirty and savage appearance.

> ❝*Piggy wore the remainders of a pair of shorts*❞

How are the contrasts between Piggy and the others displayed in the language they use?

Can you extract from this passage a further example of what makes Piggy so <u>different</u> from the others? He is described as 'an <u>outsider</u>, not only by accent'. Piggy comes from a lower-middle class/working class background. His father is dead and his mother's whereabouts unknown. This <u>contrasts</u> with Ralph's comfortable home life and the choir's public-school upbringing.

When Ralph saw a ship sail by that might have rescued them, 'he reached inside himself for the worst word he knew'.

What does the particular word he uses tell you about his background? Piggy and Ralph show their strong love of <u>civilisation</u> as Jack moves further towards <u>savagery</u>.

After the first hunt, Jack proudly tells the others that he cut the pig's throat, and yet he 'twitched as he said it'. What does this indicate about him? What effect might the hunters' chanting have upon them? (Think of a football crowd.)

At this moment, Jack and Ralph are <u>worlds</u> <u>apart</u> in both experience and emotion. Jack is jubilant after his first hunting success. Ralph is in <u>bitter</u> <u>despair</u> at the lost chance of rescue. How important is rescue to Jack now?

> **❝Piggy's glasses flew off and tinkled on the rocks.❞**

Throughout the book, Piggy shows that clear sight comes not only from the eyes but also from the mind. Piggy sees the boys' situation clearly. His glasses are a symbol of <u>understanding</u> <u>and</u> <u>reason</u>.

The success of the hunt has released Jack from the civilised need to keep back his <u>aggressive</u> tendencies, and he strikes Piggy, breaking his glasses. Both Piggy and Ralph accused him of being irresponsible, so why does Jack hit only Piggy? The breaking of one lens of the glasses symbolises the beginning of the loss of reasonable behaviour on the island.

Jack can be described as an atavist. This is someone who reverts to the behaviour and attitudes of their <u>distant</u> <u>ancestors</u>. Jack redirects his aggression from the pig to Piggy, smashing one of his lenses.

Golding wrote that the civilisation on the island 'breaks down in blood and terror because the boys are suffering from the terrible disease of being human'. As you read the novel, notice how the disease takes hold and grows worse.

66 *You didn't hunt.* 99

In the face of Jack's cruel refusal to give Piggy any meat, Simon shares his. Simon's action here is <u>kind</u> <u>and</u> <u>civilised</u> so why does he 'lower his face in shame'? What is the significance of Ralph standing with his hands full of meat 'among the ashes of the signal fire'?

As Jack and the hunters describe their first kill, they use words which show they are <u>revelling</u> in the knowledge that they deliberately spilled the pig's blood. Notice that the excuse for <u>killing</u> – that the boys need meat – is not the real reason for it. Jack likes killing for its own sake because it gives him a <u>sense</u> <u>of</u> <u>power</u>. Remember that earlier, Jack was so excited about the slaughter of the pig that he felt no guilt for letting the signal fire go out.

Explore

Why do you think Ralph now decides to call a meeting, 'even if we have to go on into the dark'? Think about why this might be one of his greatest mistakes.

Jack and his group take up a ritual <u>chant</u>: 'Kill the pig. Cut her throat. Bash her in.' Notice that Jack's rage is described as 'elemental and awe-inspiring'. In the silence that follows he 'looked round for understanding but found only respect'. Understanding and reason are being replaced by more 'elemental' forces on the island.

Uncover the plot

Delete two of the three alternatives given, to find the correct plot.

1   *While evacuating children from a war zone, a plane/a parachutist/an atom bomb crashes on a remote tropical island.*

2   *Ralph blows a megaphone/trumpet/conch shell to frighten wild animals/gather up the rest of the survivors/attract rescuers.*

3   *The group of boys elect Piggy/Ralph/Jack as their leader; this annoys Jack, the shy/confident/blond leader of the choir, but he is appeased when Ralph volunteers the choir as the army/fire tenders/hunters.*

4   *Another meeting is called, at which it is decided that the conch should give the person holding/blowing/smashing it the right to speak; some of the smaller ones describe their fear of a 'beastie' that comes out of the jungle at night.*

5   *Jack paints his face and takes the choir, who are supposed to be tending the fire, on a hunt. The fire goes out/will not light/burns up the forest and a storm/ship/plane passes in the distance.*

6   *There is a tense confrontation when the hunters return, during which Jack attacks Ralph/Piggy/Simon and breaks his glasses. Matters are partially resolved as they roast and eat the pig, and Ralph calls another meeting.*

Who? What? Why? Where? How?

1   *What does Piggy hope the boys will not do?*

2   *Why do the boys choose Ralph as their leader?*

3   *How do Jack, Ralph and Simon react to their encounter with the piglet?*

4   *What compulsion begins to 'swallow Jack up'?*

5   *Where does Simon go to on his own?*

6   *How do the smaller boys spend their days?*

7   *What stops Roger from hitting Henry with the stones?*

8   *Who gives meat to Piggy, and why does he then 'lower his face in shame'?*

Chapters 5–8

Chapter 5

Ralph is the character in the novel who learns the most. Here he asks himself some difficult questions about appearance, perception and reality, even though 'speculation was so foreign to him'. At times Ralph finds he is no longer <u>sure</u> of his own standards. Sometimes he cannot think straight. Does Ralph's clarity of thought improve as the novel progresses?

Ralph recognises Piggy's value as a <u>thinker</u>. Which words show that Ralph now understands it is a mistake to judge people and things by their <u>appearances</u>? Ralph finds himself thinking more deeply than he is accustomed to. What conclusion does he come to at this stage about Piggy?

❝*This meeting must not be fun, but business.* ❞

As the boys take their places for the assembly, notice which group chooses to sit on Ralph's right and who sits to his left. Can you see the significance here? Think about the terms 'left' and 'right' as used in modern politics.

Ralph <u>lectures</u> the boys on their unsanitary habits – they are soiling their own living areas. What does this indicate about the state of their civilisation? Ralph says that they ought to die before they let the fire go out: 'the fire is the most important thing'.

Ralph is still closely connected to the adult world of <u>order</u> and <u>stability</u>. Do you think that this is why he has a struggle to understand why things change? Do you think that Jack's

Text commentary

increasing power over the others is helped by a flaw in Ralph's leadership? If so, what is it? If you think Ralph has no flaws in the way he leads the boys, what is it that goes wrong? Does he make a mistake?

Ralph tries to erase the littluns' fears by talking sensibly, but Jack ruins this. Jack tells the littluns that fear is within them all and they must learn to live with it. Jack seems to want to make the others believe in the beast. How could this be of help to him?

Piggy has a typically rational argument against being afraid. Can you say why he feels this way? After all, he is particularly physically vulnerable. You might have expected him to be the most afraid. But Piggy is trying to remove the boys' fear while Jack is trying to reinforce it. What does this reveal about their different characters?

Piggy believes that science has the answer to fear and superstition. This illustrates Piggy's 'adult' clear-sightedness and his civilised way of thinking. Notice the irony of Piggy's use of the 'double negative'. This is the difference between what he says and what he means. He says 'I know there isn't no beast ... but I know there isn't no fear either'; but 'is not no beast' and 'is not no fear' actually mean that there is a beast and there is fear. When Piggy and, later, Simon suggest that the thing to fear is lodged within themselves, they are voicing one of the fundamental themes of the novel.

❝A whiteness in the gloom❞

Simon, although self-conscious, feels 'a perilous necessity to speak'. He tries to explain his feeling that the beast may be inside them. 'Humankind's essential illness' is the evil force within man. Simon is struggling to find a way to explain this. He is ridiculed by Jack and his group. What does this suggest about the way society treats the mystic or prophet? Was this assembly a mistake?

Much of Chapter 5 is concerned with discussing fear and the beast. Notice that fear makes the boys more <u>irrational</u> as darkness falls. Do you agree with Ralph that he 'was wrong to call this assembly so late'?

Ralph's failure to keep order is partly his fault and partly the fault of others. Which mistakes does Ralph know he has made? Are there any he is not aware of? Why does Ralph become unpopular?

Look at Piggy's speech, where he separates himself from the boys' irrational behaviour and beliefs: 'I didn't vote for no ghosts!' Jack's response shows his total disregard for Piggy.

66*Bollocks to the rules!*99

The assembly and the conch are <u>dismissed</u> in this one phrase. Jack challenges Ralph's suitability for the leadership. Ralph responds by telling Jack he is 'breaking the rules'. This is a point of crisis in the novel. Does Ralph's faith in <u>democratic</u> behaviour now strike you as ridiculous? Think about when the novel was written. Jack's shout: 'Bollocks to the rules!' brings into the open his changing character and intentions.

Explore
Re-read what Jack thought about rules in Chapter 1. How has he changed? What is he challenging now?

Bear in mind that Golding was concerned about the way many people were thinking after the Second World War had ended. He wrote: 'You think that now the war is over and an evil thing destroyed, you are safe because you are naturally kind and decent. But I know why the thing rose in Germany. I know it could happen in any country. It could happen here.'

> **He hates me. I dunno why.**

Piggy speaks of his fear – <u>fear</u> <u>of</u> <u>people</u>. He recognises that the <u>bully</u> in Jack could lead to danger for himself. Why is it that Piggy understands more about the way people behave than Ralph does?

Ralph's wish about grown-ups: 'If only they could get a message to us' and his desire for a 'sign or something' acknowledges the need for adult authority.

Chapter 6

> **Yard by yard, puff by puff**

Explore

Ralph is often associated with yellow – the colour of the sun. Can you think why this might be appropriate? (Think about why it is appropriate that Jack is often associated with red and black.)

The dead parachutist is the 'sign' for which Ralph asked in the last chapter, but is not, perhaps, the one he would have preferred. The fact that the adult is dead gives us a hint about the condition of the world <u>away</u> <u>from</u> <u>the</u> <u>island</u>.

Jack openly refuses to recognise the <u>authority</u> <u>of</u> <u>the</u> <u>conch</u>. Which phrase suggests that he considers the actions of the hunters to be outside the control of the assembly?

With the arrival of the parachutist, the idea of a beast has been given a <u>physical</u> <u>form</u>. But on the hunt to find it, Simon feels 'a flicker of incredulity'. There follows a good example of his intuitive intelligence, his 'inward sight'. Why do you think Simon's 'picture of a human' is described as being both 'heroic and sick'?

66 *What a place for a fort!* 99

Castle Rock eventually becomes a fortress for Jack's tribe. Why is this place a suitable setting for <u>savagery</u> and <u>superstition</u>? What does Ralph think of it?

Explore

Compare this personification with the description near the start of Chapter 4, when Golding describes 'the other side' of the island.

Notice how Golding uses personification to describe the sea; that is, he describes it as a living thing: 'the swell … seemed like the breathing of some stupendous creature'.

Jack joins Ralph on the hunt for the beast. Why are these moments of conversation between the two boys so touching, so poignant? What breaks it up? Which event towards the end of the chapter hints at things to come?

Chapter 7

66 *A little fall of the heart* 99

Notice Ralph's concern about his filthy condition. A little further on he experiences 'a little fall of the heart'. This phrase suggests that he has begun to mind his dirty and unkempt appearance. Ralph's behaviour is <u>deteriorating</u> – he bites his nails, he daydreams, he becomes forgetful. Why do you think this is?

Notice the <u>contrast</u> of the 'other side of the island' to their own side. The opposite side of the island is 'utterly different' because the cold sea hardens the images. There are no 'mirages' here, instead the horizon is a 'hard, clipped blue'. On their side the lagoon protects them and 'one might dream of rescue'. Why does the lagoon side encourage daydreams?

Notice the language used by Golding to describe the sea on this side of the island. What is the effect of words like 'suck', 'sink', 'plaster down', 'rise', 'roar' and 'irresistibly'? The two sides of the island are rather like the two 'sides' of human beings – the good and the evil. The action has moved away from the 'friendly side' of both.

> **"Simon was speaking almost in his ear."**

How far do you consider Simon's words to Ralph to be prophetic? When Ralph calls Simon 'batty', what does this tell us about his understanding of Simon? If Ralph does not value what Simon says, will anyone else?

Notice that Simon speaks very softly to Ralph, 'almost in his ear' – like an inner voice, or perhaps the voice of conscience? Contrast this with the way Jack speaks.

Ralph's dreams of his old home cannot help him cope with his present situation. The images of books suggest a child's ideas of travel, adventure and fear. But this is the view from the comfort of a normal, civilised life. How different is Ralph now from when he used to read these books? Why do you think Ralph needs to remind himself of his old life?

The 'play' hunt with Robert as the boar has a noticeable effect on Ralph. Think carefully about the sentence, 'the desire to squeeze and hurt was overmastering'. What is Golding suggesting here? Notice again the chant and its effect.

Berengaria was the wife of Richard the Lionheart. She is credited with saving her husband's life by sucking a wound made by a poisoned arrow. Is there an ominous ring to Simon's comment about Berengaria? Think about the symbolism which surrounds Simon and the word 'wound'. Now think about how Jack and the idea of wounding are related in the novel.

"'Just a game,' said Ralph uneasily.'"

In his own mind, Ralph tries to keep what is happening on the same level as play, like a rugby game. Rugby is a game that in a <u>secure</u> <u>world</u> is played <u>strictly</u> <u>to</u> <u>the</u> <u>rules</u>. Play on the island develops into something different. What do you think makes Ralph say, 'Just a game'? Why does he say this 'uneasily'?

Jack and his hunters plan a mock hunt – a <u>ritual</u> <u>performance</u>. How can you tell that the evil, sadistic elements within them are coming out? Look carefully at what is said, especially about using a littlun.

Simon offers to go back alone through the dark jungle. This is important. If he had stayed and seen the beast with the others he might have established the truth. Look at how Jack talks 'in a queer tight voice' about not letting anything happen to Piggy. Ralph feels Jack's 'antagonism'. The tension between the two boys builds up during the trek.

"I'm going up the mountain to look for the beast… coming?"

Notice all the references to <u>darkness</u> during this trip. Ralph has learned by experience not to undertake things in the dark. (When?) Notice how Jack tests Ralph. Roger, whom we already know to be <u>destructive</u>, is one of those present on the climb to find the 'beast'. Simon is no longer there. What does this tell us about the shifting of power from Ralph to Jack and his hunters?

Although Ralph's leadership is <u>disintegrating</u>, he does not lack courage – but everybody flees from the 'beast'. Golding's description of the decomposing parachutist skilfully merges the two concepts of beast and human; 'Something like a great ape' he calls it, with 'the ruin of a face'. Notice this subtle echo of the <u>masks</u> worn by the hunters.

Chapter 8

> ❝*The beast had teeth,' said Ralph, 'and big black eyes.'* ❞

Ralph is now convinced of the <u>reality</u> of the beast. What is the effect of the symbolism and coincidence in Ralph's comment, 'And now that thing squats by the fire as though it didn't want us to be rescued–'? Would the effect have been different if the parachutist had landed on the beach, or in the scar, or on top of Castle Rock? It is important that the 'beast' appears on the mountain top. Why?

> ❝*I've called an assembly*❞

Jack takes the <u>initiative</u> in formally calling an assembly. Is this the only time he uses the conch? Look at the words Golding uses to describe the way Jack holds the conch. Does Jack hold it like this out of respect for the authority it represents? What are his motives in calling this meeting?

Explore

Carefully study the way Jack uses the democratic procedure of the assembly to try to manipulate the group. On which of their emotions is he playing?

Why do you think the group would not vote against Ralph as leader? Does it say something about their fear of speaking out? Of whom might they be afraid?

Ralph, who seems quite a good person, does not make a particularly good leader. What makes a good leader? Think about what might have happened if Jack had been elected leader from the start: would things have turned out better, or worse? Ralph tries to keep <u>order</u> by using <u>rules</u>. But people do not always keep to the rules. How do you imagine Jack and his choir would have kept order?

"I'm not going to play any longer."

Consider the irony of Jack's words. Play has been transformed from something harmless into a hysterical ritual. Yet there is pathos here too: can you identify exactly why Jack's comment is so touching?

How does Simon display self-sacrifice here? Even Piggy cannot understand the point Simon is making. Only Simon is able to recognise that this is the turning-point in their lives on the island. Notice the way the group does not respect or recognise Simon's value.

Explore

How has the assembly's opinion of Piggy changed now that Jack has left? Contrast Piggy's intellect with that of Simon. Piggy is intensely practical. How would you describe the way Simon thinks?

Piggy has assisted with the building of the new fire. He even lights the fire himself. This is important, because it shows that Piggy is no longer an outsider. Why is this?

Some of the other boys have left the group, presumably to join Jack. Piggy's humour is ironic: 'I expect they won't play either'. Which boys are the first to go? Can you see why? The boys prepare a 'feast' for Ralph. Compare this feast with Jack's in Chapter 9.

"in front of Simon, the Lord of the Flies hung on his stick and grinned"

Simon retreats to his private den. Notice his mood of self-denial. Compare Simon at this point with Christ in the wilderness. What did they both have ahead of them? In his private place, Simon is surrounded by nature. Notice the butterfly – a symbol of delicate perfection in air. Look at which form of insect life displays itself to Simon the next time we see him in his den.

Sample response

Compare the characters of Jack and Ralph in *Lord of the Flies*.

Ralph and Jack are the two oldest boys on the island and so they both appear as leader-figures to the others. However, they are very different characters in how they think and behave.✓

Ralph is twelve years old, well-built, fair-haired and comes from a solid middle-class background.✓ His father is a naval commander. Ralph has a very strong sense of fair play and is well-balanced and decent and so presents a hero-type figure. ✓ Jack, on the other hand, is a quite different character. He asserts his claim to leadership right from the start. The harsh side of his character can be seen straight away when he arrives with the choir. He gives them orders and treats them strictly, making them stand to attention in the tremendous heat even though they do not like it: 'Wearily obedient, the choir huddled into line and stood there swaying in the sun.'✓

Jack is obviously a boy who is used to being obeyed. Golding's physical description of him seems to confirm his unpleasant character: 'His face was crumpled and freckled, and ugly without silliness.' It is significant that he wears a black cap, like an executioner.✓

Jack and Ralph come into conflict right from the start, although at first it is not a violent conflict. Jack announces, 'I ought to be chief', but it is suggested that the thing is put to the vote.✓ When Ralph is voted in Jack is obviously angry: 'the freckles on his face disappeared under a blush of mortification'. Ralph, though, shows his leadership skills by giving Jack command of the choir and telling him that he and the choir can be the hunters.✓

As time goes on Ralph (assisted by Piggy) shows his practical side and tries to get the boys organised by building shelters, ✓ setting up a signal fire and so on. Jack, though, is only interested in hunting and he is developing an unhealthy obsession with blood and killing. ✓ Ralph tries to keep to the rules of a civilised society and treats people fairly and sensitively. Jack gets more and more out of control, though, becoming more and more of a savage, painting his face and daubing others with blood from the pig they killed. ✓

In the end Jack breaks away from Ralph's group and, through fear because of threats and intimidation, most of the other boys join him. ✓ Jack's savagery increases and all order breaks down. The killing escalates from animals to humans, as first Simon and then Piggy are killed, and Ralph himself is only saved by the arrival of the naval officer. ✓

Ralph stands for civilised values and democracy, and is decent and fair, but Jack stands for tyranny and dictatorship ruled by fear, torture and killing. In the end savagery triumphs over civilisation. ✓

Examiner's comments

This is a high-quality response which shows a clear understanding of the characters of Ralph and Jack and an excellent understanding of the text overall. Textual references are used effectively to support the ideas, and quotations are woven well into the fabric of the essay. Mention of Ralph and the conch would have been useful, but the response shows a good understanding of the symbolic importance of both characters in the wider thematic context of the novel as a whole.

Quick quiz answers

Quick quiz 1
Uncover the plot
1 a plane
2 conch shell; gather up the rest of the survivors
3 Ralph; confident; hunters
4 holding
5 goes out; ship
6 Piggy

Who? What? Why? Where? How?
1 call him by his former nickname, Piggy
2 for his stillness, his size, his attractive appearance, and because he possesses the conch
3 They all rush forward and Jack raises his knife, but he cannot bring himself to commit the 'enormity' of hurting a living creature.
4 the compulsion to track down and kill
5 to a hideaway in the jungle
6 eating and playing on the beach
7 a taboo of civilisation remaining from the old life – the invisible protection of parents, school, policemen and the law
8 Simon; perhaps because he has shown compassion, therefore laying himself open to mockery and showing himself different from 'the group'.

Quick quiz 2
Uncover the plot
1 Ralph; human nature'
2 a dead parachutist; Sam 'n' Eric; have seen the beast
3 with the littluns

4 Jack; Ralph's
5 falls into a trance
6 head; Lord of the Flies

Who? What? Why? How?
1 He is astonished by a sudden 'strange mood of speculation'.
2 He realises that Piggy has brains and can think.
3 that the coconut shells should have been filled with water; the shelters are inadequate; the boys are no longer using the rocks as a lavatory as agreed; that the fire should never go out, and never be taken from the mountain; and that they should talk about their fears
4 He feels he must explain his conviction that the beast is a part of them; the evil in human nature.
5 to 'where he came from'
6 Roger
7 that they are 'boys armed with sticks' – hunting is Jack's 'trade', his obsession; by insulting his hunters Ralph is striking at what Jack holds most dear
8 he means 'why is everything going wrong, and breaking up'; with Ralph's new-found understanding he respects Piggy's brains and intuition

Quick quiz 3
Uncover the plot
1 climbs the mountain; 'the beast'
2 join; Simon; group
3 Jack; tyrannical
4 raids; Piggy's glasses; four

5   *are captured; Roger; escapes*

6   *the savages*

What? When? Why? How?

1   *to release the dead man from the indignity of being pulled about by the wind*

2   *painted and garlanded, 'like an idol'*

3   *The wind lifts him and carries him out to sea.*

4   *to 'steal' fire*

5   *a cooking fire, not a signal fire*

6   *when Jack orders his tribe to capture the twins*

7   *never*

8   *Golding says he weeps for 'the end of innocence, the darkness of man's heart, and the fall through the air of the true, wise friend called Piggy'.*

Published by Letts Educational
An imprint of HarperCollins*Publishers*
77–85 Fulham Palace Road
London W6 8JB

Telephone: 0844 576 8126
Fax: 0844 576 8131
Email: education@harpercollins.co.uk
Website: www.lettsandlonsdale.com

First published 1994
Revised edition 2004

ISBN 978 1 84315 315 3

9

06/091110

Text © 1994 John Mahoney and Stewart Martin
2004 edition revised by Steven Croft

Design and illustration © Letts Educational

Cover and text design by Hardlines Ltd., Charlbury, Oxfordshire.
Typeset by Letterpart Ltd., Reigate, Surrey.
Graphic illustration by Beehive Illustration, Cirencester, Gloucestershire.
Commissioned by Cassandra Birmingham
Editorial project management by Jo Kemp

British Library Cataloguing in Publication Data.
A CIP record of this book is available from the British Library.

Printed in China

In the meantime, the choir has undergone a <u>change</u>. Not long ago, 'their voices had been the song of angels'. What have the choir now become? What do you think is the significance of the black caps they retain? (Think of what British judges sometimes used to wear on their heads, and when.) Jack tells the group, 'I'm going to be chief'. What does this indicate about the <u>political organisation</u> of Jack's tribe?

Jack's surname is Merridew. The name means 'lord of the place'. It is significant that this is the name Jack first wanted to be called by. It is not difficult to think of Jack as the <u>villain</u> of the novel, but is this altogether fair? Was Jack to blame for the death of the littlun with the birthmark? Is it only Jack who is responsible for Simon's death? Who is to blame for Piggy's death?

Explore

Try to decide whether Jack actually knows when he is doing wrong, or whether he is just unable to resist 'the beast' for as long as the others.

The hunters are in passionate <u>agreement</u> with Jack's proposals. How does he release them from 'the depths of their tormented private lives'? Jack proposes a primitive and superstitious way of <u>appeasing</u> the beast. This marks a further stage in his <u>degeneration</u>. Jack finds that <u>rituals</u> are important to him. For example, how do you think he feels during the episodes of chanting and dancing?

❝The pigs lay, bloated bags of fat❞

Pink is an important colour image; it often makes an <u>ironic contrast</u> with the action. Here, the 'pink' of the pigs suggests a baby, a vulnerable thing. Look also at the use of pink to describe the island and the conch in Chapter 1. Read carefully the description of the attack and the killing of the sow. Would a real hunter kill a sow with young?

Golding's description of the sow's killing is electrified with <u>forceful</u> <u>emotion</u>: 'wedded to her in lust', 'fulfilled upon her'. Why do you think he uses sexual terminology?

The hunt of the sow can be seen as the point when the boys finally <u>break</u> with their past moral values and innocence. Why is hope for civilised life on the island lost from this moment? The force of <u>destruction</u>, represented by Jack, <u>triumphs</u> over the <u>controls</u> of <u>civilisation</u>, represented by Ralph.

The violence of war, or the hunt, makes the act of killing <u>thrilling</u>. It releases the hidden, evil side from humankind's inner being. Golding thought evil much more common than many people like to believe.

❝Roger began to withdraw his spear❞

The name Roger means 'famous with the spear'. Notice Golding's interpretation of this in Roger's actions. Think about Roger's part in killing the sow. What evidence can you find that Roger is particularly <u>sadistic</u>?

In a <u>primitive</u> <u>celebration</u> of killing, Jack rubs blood over Maurice's face. This is a further example of Jack's commitment to the <u>savage</u> <u>life</u>. By killing the sow, Jack and his band have symbolically killed a mother/parent figure. From this moment on, they are <u>savage</u> and <u>brutal</u>. Their <u>innocence</u> is lost. Think about which characters are absent from the hunt. Do they keep their innocence? The hunters relish their release from civilised behaviour, illustrated here by their language. They are now free to say words like 'ass'.

Roger calls Jack 'Chief' for the first time. Does the tribe ever again refer to him as Jack? The pig's head is stuck on a prepared stake and left as a gift for the beast. Roger later sharpens another stick: how similar is its intended use?

> **"'You are a silly little boy,' said the Lord of the Flies."**

The strange conversation Simon has with the Lord of the Flies can be interpreted as a <u>symbolic</u> experience; a <u>conflict</u> between good and evil. Is Simon's conversation with evil real or imagined? Do not worry if you cannot decide. Golding wants you to consider the conversation from all angles, so you should try to find a variety of interpretations.

Explore

What does Golding mean when he says that Simon's gaze 'was held by that ancient, inescapable recognition'?

Simon has turned this part of the jungle into a symbolic <u>church</u>. The beast is on the mountain, and the hunters bring before Simon (without knowing that he is there) what Golding has called 'their false god'. But the false god of the hunters knows Simon is there. A pulse begins to beat in Simon's head. What suggestion is there in the text that Simon may be having an epileptic fit during his conversation with the Lord of the Flies?

The pig's head rules the flies just as the evil inside the boys controls their actions. Flies feed upon the sow's head, just as the boys have begun to feed on the pigs of the island. What else do the boys almost begin to feed on at the end of the novel?

> **"Lord of the Flies"**

Golding's frequent use of <u>parallels</u> and echoes throughout the novel sometimes includes references to other stories, myths or legends. The name 'Lord of the Flies' is given to the pig's head on a stick by Golding, not by the boys. The name is a literal translation of Beelzebub, the name of the <u>devil</u> in the Bible.

Simon's <u>intuitive</u> understanding of the nature of being human enables him to envisage a world which is full of <u>wonder</u> and at

the same time full of <u>dangers</u>. This is why he can still like Jack. This is why the evil represented as the Lord of the Flies must try to beat Simon. The Lord of the Flies knows Simon's <u>inner feelings</u>. In what way is he trying to win the battle with Simon when he says, 'You like Ralph a lot, don't you? And Piggy, and Jack?'

In the confrontation between the Lord of the Flies and Simon, notice the <u>parallel</u> with the Bible story of Christ being tempted in the wilderness. Does this help you with yet another interpretation of Simon's 'liking' Jack? The Lord of the Flies tries to persuade Simon that evil in humans is so strong that resistance is useless. Does Simon accept this?

❝*The laughter shivered again*❞

Why do you think Golding makes the Lord of the Flies speak 'in the voice of a <u>schoolmaster</u>'? Are Simon's 'times' a reference to fits, or to moments of sudden understanding, as in a vision? Perhaps they are both. By the end of Simon's dialogue with the Lord of the Flies, in how many ways can you interpret the 'blackness that spread'? Look at the phrase 'we shall do you' and notice how it includes Ralph and Piggy. Why is this, do you suppose?

Quick quiz 2

Uncover the plot

Delete two of the three alternatives given, to find the correct plot.

1 Jack/Piggy/Ralph, burdened by unaccustomed insights into his past/human nature/how to hunt, calls another meeting.

2 An injured parachutist/a rescue party/a dead parachutist drops onto the island; Ralph and Jack/Sam 'n' Eric/Roger and Simon, tending the fire, see it and believe that they are about to be rescued/have seen the beast/have seen a ghost.

3 Jack and Ralph lead a search to find the beast, leaving Piggy with the littluns/alone/with the parachutist.

4 Ralph/Piggy/Jack calls a meeting and calls Ralph's/Jack's/Roger's leadership into question; when none of the boys respond he leaves, humiliated and enraged.

5 Simon's suggestion that they climb the mountain again is mocked, and he goes to his private place where he falls into a trance/is attacked/dies.

6 Jack's 'tribe' hunt and kill a pig and leave its ass/head/corpse on a stick as a gift to the beast. In Simon's trance it speaks to him as the Lord of the Flies/Sam 'n' Eric/Bill, the beast of evil within man.

Who? What? Why? How?

1 Walking to the evening meeting, why is Ralph 'overcome with astonishment'?

2 What does Ralph realise about Piggy?

3 What points does Ralph make at the meeting?

4 Why does Simon feel a 'perilous necessity' to speak? What does he think the beast is?

5 According to Simon, where will Ralph get back to?

6 Who joins Ralph and Jack in the 'mad expedition' up the mountain?

7 What does Ralph say about Jack's hunters, and why does Piggy say 'Now you done it.'?

8 What does Ralph mean when he asks Piggy 'what's wrong', and why does he ask Piggy?

Quick quiz

49

Chapters 9–12

Chapter 9

> ❝'What else is there to do?'❞

How does Simon's question show that his confrontation with the Lord of the Flies has not weakened his <u>quest</u> <u>for</u> <u>truth</u>? On what previous occasion has Simon spoken these words? At the summit of the mountain, Simon has seen what 'the beast' really is. It is only a dead man. This incident shows how <u>accurate</u> both Piggy and Simon have been in their understanding that in some way fear comes from inside humans.

Simon shows saintly <u>compassion</u> in freeing the parachute's lines. He looks down from the mountain onto the camp. Like Moses in the Bible, Simon will bring the truth down from the mountain only to find that his people have become <u>degenerate</u> and have fallen to worshipping false gods.

> ❝I don't like them clouds.❞

Explore

Jack is now 'painted and garlanded', sitting like 'an idol'. What does this tell you about his leadership? In what tone of voice does he speak to his tribe?

The approach of darkness and the storm is made to suggest the coming <u>horror</u>. In the light of what is about to happen, notice the <u>irony</u> of Piggy's excuse for going to Jack's feast.

Even after the boys have <u>split</u> into two camps, they are <u>united</u> for a moment in <u>making</u> <u>fun</u> of Piggy. Notice all the references at this point to laughter.

What indications are there that Jack rules his tribe by <u>fear</u>? Can you think why Jack has to rule by force and fear? Notice that Jack wishes them to be afraid not of himself, but of a much older

Text commentary

enemy: the evil within all humans. Jack wins new followers through a mixture of fear and promises of a higher standard of living (pig meat).

Against the growth of <u>tyranny</u>, the law-abiding population – symbolised by Ralph, Piggy and Simon – is helpless. They do not realise until it is too late that Jack's followers have no <u>respect</u> for lawful society.

When Jack invites the others to join his tribe, Ralph replies: 'I'm chief' and says: 'I've got the conch'. How much does the word 'tremulously' tell you about Ralph's position? By asking who wants to have 'fun', is Jack deliberately <u>manipulating</u> the others, or is he simply being irresponsible?

❝The dark sky was shattered❞

Jack answers Ralph's appeal to sense and logic with the <u>ritual frenzy</u> of the dance. The chant becomes sinister. Compare its words with those of the chant in Chapter 4. Why have they changed? The lightning and the chant whip the tribe into a frenzy. Where are Ralph and Piggy at this stage? Notice Golding's language; the circle of screaming, savage boys has become a single organism – <u>the</u> <u>real</u> <u>beast</u>.

Simon is trying to tell the boys about the beast, even while he is being battered to death. Notice the biblical echo of the Crucifixion in the mention of a dead man on a hill.

Those who see the <u>truth</u> <u>of</u> <u>the</u> <u>situation</u>, like Simon, and those who are on the side of what is right and good, like Piggy, are subjected to 'the shrill screaming that rose before the beast'. What effect is Golding creating by calling Simon 'the beast' in this scene? The actions of 'the beast' (Simon) are pitifully human –

it is still trying to explain the truth. The crowd is like a pack of savage, crazed animals. Just as Simon dies, the dead parachutist drifts out to sea and vanishes.

Could Simon have done anything to prevent his own death? If the other boys had listened to him, would they have been saved from savagery? Or does Simon have to die before the boys can be saved? Is this the point of the story of the Crucifixion of Jesus?

The colour imagery used in connection with Simon changes after his death. What is Simon's colour now? Is Piggy correct to reject the use of the word 'murder' in connection with Simon's killing? Golding's language makes Simon's death beautiful: 'Somewhere over the darkened curve of the world…'. The sea takes Simon's body 'softly', and merges it with the energies of the natural world. Why is this a fitting end for him?

Chapter 10

❝Call an assembly?❞

Ralph laughs at the suggestion that they should call an assembly. Can you identify the emotion which causes Ralph to laugh? He describes Simon's death as 'murder'. Why does he feel the need to do this? Note that Piggy, the thinker, cannot bring himself to think about the terrible deed: 'We can't do no good thinking about it, see?'

Piggy's explanation for the ritual killing of Simon is that they were 'scared'. Ralph is searching for a way to explain an entirely different emotion. Can you define this emotion? Ralph reacts to Simon's murder by regressing momentarily into infancy. Piggy tries to convince Ralph that Simon's

death was an <u>accident</u>. He uses his poor eyesight to excuse his <u>moral</u> <u>blindness</u>. Why is he being dishonest? How does this fit in with Piggy's usual common sense?

Sam 'n' Eric appear dragging a big log out of the forest. Ralph calls to them. Look at the words 'They flushed and looked past him into the air'. Ralph, Piggy and Sam 'n' Eric are trying to cope with the <u>guilt</u> they feel for taking part in Simon's <u>ritual</u> <u>killing</u>. This is why the word 'dance' is now 'obscene' to them all. What does their guilt tell us about them? Do you think Jack feels guilty?

Over at Castle Rock, Roger returns to the camp. Why do you think Roger considers Jack to be 'a proper Chief'? What event does this <u>foreshadow</u>? Jack's tyrannical regime allows <u>sadistic</u> actions to take place, like the promised beating of Wilfred (for which we are never given a reason).

When Roger hears that a littlun is about to be beaten and is possibly being <u>tortured</u>, he responds by 'assimilating the possibilities of irresponsible authority'. What 'possibilities' are there for <u>irresponsible</u> <u>authority</u> that are impossible for responsible authority? What does this tell you about Roger's character?

> **❝Some of you will stay here to improve the cave and defend the gate.❞**

Jack manipulates the emotions of his followers by suggesting they guard against <u>two</u> <u>dangers</u>. What are the two dangers? Jack presents an 'implication of further terrors' to his tribe – can you think of two reasons why he tells them that they didn't kill the beast after all?

Can you say why Piggy is stronger than Ralph at this point? Ralph's 'nightly game of supposing' tells you about his current state of mind. Why is Ralph's game sad?

Back on the beach, Piggy and Ralph light a fire. What does Ralph think the 'double function' of the fire is? The boys are showing clear signs of mental and emotional deterioration.

Ralph dreams of 'lamps and wheels'. These represent man's developed technology, ways in which man has triumphed over distance and darkness. Compare this with the situation on the island. What does Ralph's uncontrollable laughter tell us about him? Notice how his body 'jumped and twitched'. Compare this with Piggy's 'dignity'. Ralph's game of supposing continues in his sleep, but becomes a nightmare.

> **Desperately, Ralph prayed that the beast would prefer littluns.**

Read this section carefully, noting the reactions of Ralph and Piggy. This is the two boys' final consideration of the beast. How has their view of the beast changed since Chapter 1? Notice the way animals are initially suggested by the words 'vicious snarling' and 'biting', and how this changes to blend animals with humans, as with the word 'fingers'. The beast is no longer an unknown animal of some kind, it is human.

> **From his left hand dangled Piggy's broken glasses.**

The theft of Piggy's glasses represents the last defeat of the power of reason on the island. Which word suggests that 'the Chief' treats the glasses as a trophy from the hunt? Thieves normally steal what they (or others) value. What is revealed by the fact that the savages did not bother to steal the conch?

Chapter 11

> ❝He held out the conch to Piggy who flushed, this time with pride.❞

At the end of Chapter 10, Ralph's group are pleased to find that the conch has not been stolen. Can you think why they still use the conch? The boys' desire to 'smarten up a bit' before <u>confronting</u> the savage tribe shows that they feel the need to show 'we aren't savages really'. At this stage, do you think Ralph's group fully realise the extent of the tribe's degeneration?

> ❝Piggy! Stop a minute!❞

Piggy is <u>physically</u> helpless without his glasses, but he shows <u>extreme</u> <u>courage</u> in his decision to face Jack and demand what is 'right'. To what extent does Piggy know his own limitations? This distinguishes Piggy as more 'adult' than the other boys. Think about Piggy's strengths and weaknesses. Do the other boys dislike him only because he is fat, has asthma and wears glasses?

On their way to confront Jack they pass the place where the tribe had danced.

The twisted growth in front of Castle Rock <u>symbolises</u> the formidable task which confronts Ralph's group. There is a <u>contrast</u> between the savages, who 'appeared, painted out of recognition' and Ralph's behaviour when he tells them to 'Stop being silly!' How far does Ralph's manner towards the 'savages' mirror that of the naval officer at the end?

> **Roger advanced upon them as one wielding a nameless authority.**

Roger becomes more <u>irresponsible</u> as this incident unfolds. Think about what the 'source of power' which begins to 'pulse in Roger's body' could be. He feels this <u>growing power</u> as he becomes aware of the <u>vulnerability</u> of the boys on the ledge beneath. Significantly, Piggy is now kneeling.

Ralph demands Piggy's glasses back and responds to Jack's 'Who says?' with 'I say!' He shows great courage when <u>confronting</u> the tribe. How can you tell that his speech will be ineffectual? He uses schoolboy language: 'You aren't playing the game'. However, the group are now savages, no longer schoolboys.

> **I said 'grab them!**

At the moment of their capture, Sam 'n' Eric 'protested out of the heart of civilisation'. How is this explained by what they say? Ralph's temper breaks at this. 'You're a beast and a swine and a bloody, bloody thief!' is another example of schoolboy language, but notice the irony of the words 'beast' and 'swine'.

Golding uses the <u>onomatopoeic</u> word 'Zup!' to describe Roger's stone-throwing. (Onomatopoeic words are those which are invented to resemble the sound of the action or thing that they describe.) How does this word reduce the threat of 'his one hand still on the lever'? Roger's position gives him an unusual view of Ralph and Piggy. The words Golding uses to describe the way Roger sees them have a particular effect. What is this?

> **You're acting like a crowd of kids.**

Piggy is <u>brave</u> enough to speak out right up to the moment of his death. Ralph adds to Piggy's plea for rational behaviour. 'Which is better,' he says, 'law and rescue' or 'breaking things

up?' Ralph has used these last words before (in Chapters 5 and 8) to describe the <u>disintegration</u> of <u>civilised</u> <u>order</u>. Find them, and think about how Ralph's view of life on the island has altered since the beginning of the novel.

Roger experiences 'a sense of delirious abandonment'. This reveals the extent to which Roger has become a <u>mindless</u> <u>savage</u>.

How does the word <u>'talisman'</u> add to our sadness at the description of the conch in its last moments before it is smashed? The <u>destruction</u> of the fragile conch <u>symbolises</u> how easily <u>democracy</u> can be <u>overthrown</u>.

Explore

Study the description of Piggy's death and the way his body is washed out to sea. It is cold, hard, impersonal. Compare this with the description of Simon's death. Why did Golding adopt two different approaches to these similar events?

Notice the colour of the rock onto which Piggy falls. The scene suggests a <u>sacrifice</u> on a primitive altar. Now look at the use of <u>personification</u> in 'the sea breathed again in a long, slow sigh'. How does this affect your response to Piggy's death? There is <u>irony</u> in: 'Piggy, saying nothing, with no time for even a grunt, travelled through the air…'. Why does Golding make Piggy an object to laugh at even at the moment of his death?

> **❝The hangman's horror clung round him❞**

The conch and Piggy are destroyed at the <u>same</u> <u>time</u>. This represents the complete destruction of <u>rationality</u>. After Piggy's murder, Ralph is unable to speak: 'no sound came'. This suggests that intelligent communication has broken down. We are witnessing the birth of a new world, based on the call of the beast, in which the most powerful form of communication is the <u>chant</u>. This reverses the way the world begins in the Bible (John I): 'In the beginning was the Word…'

What do you think is the 'nameless authority' which Roger now wields?

Roger is no longer <u>restrained</u> by civilised patterns of behaviour (remember in Chapter 4 he found himself unable to throw stones directly at Henry). Sam 'n' Eric are to be '<u>persuaded</u>' to join Jack's tribe. It is implied that they are <u>tortured</u>.

Chapter 12

❝ *Ralph lay in a covert, wondering about his wounds.* ❞

Ralph's <u>acceptance</u> of the <u>reality</u> of life on the island is shown in the words 'But really, this was not Bill. This was a savage…'. He still has fleeting moments of <u>hope</u> that they are just boys playing a game: he thinks of symbols of normal civilised behaviour like obeying teachers, wearing caps and claiming 'pax' (literally peace, the old-fashioned term for safety in children's games). However, his hope for safety is <u>absurd</u>. What do you understand by the 'indefinable connection between himself and Jack'? How are Ralph and Jack connected?

Compare Ralph's and Simon's encounters with the Lord of the Flies. Why did Ralph feel 'sick fear and rage'? And why is it that the skull 'won't tell'?

Although Ralph smashes the skull, its 'grin' grows larger. He cannot wipe out the evil which the skull symbolises.

In realising that he is an '<u>outcast</u>', Ralph joins Piggy and Simon. Look at the words he uses to explain this. Notice how they echo Piggy's language.

❝ *It's only me. Ralph.* ❞

Sam 'n' Eric are <u>enslaved</u> by a 'new and shameful loyalty'. They represent <u>oppressed</u> people, whose only safety lies in joining the <u>stronger</u> group. How do they help, but also betray, Ralph? Why do they eventually betray him? How would you have reacted in their position?

Sam 'n' Eric tell Ralph about the plan to <u>hunt</u> <u>him</u> <u>down</u> like a pig. What does this hunt suggest about the depths to which the boys have sunk? Notice Roger's part in the torture. Does he seem <u>worse</u> than Jack? It is Roger who has 'sharpened a stick at both ends' in <u>preparation</u> for Ralph's death. Think about when such a stick was last used.

Look at the <u>imagery</u> which is used to describe Ralph during the final hunt. This develops during the hunt itself until he finally 'bursts' out of the jungle 'screaming, snarling, bloody'. Ralph uses <u>animal</u> <u>tactics</u> to survive the hunt. This hunt, with its line of pursuers, mirrors the children's playground game of 'chain-he' or 'tag'. Why is this echo of a 'game' intensely <u>ironic</u>?

"Now the fire was nearer"

Ralph's sense of <u>responsibility</u> is illustrated by his comment that the boys are fools, and by his question 'what would they eat tomorrow'?

When Ralph at last notices that the stick he took from the pig's head 'was sharpened at both ends' he becomes aware of the implications. Will the hunters merely kill him? The pig's head was on the stick. What did the savages do with the rest of the animal? Ralph's inner voice recalls Simon's prophecy. Does he now think Simon was 'batty'?

"Ralph screamed"

The idea of the hunt, developed throughout the book, reaches a <u>climax</u> with the manhunt for Ralph. Reduced to an animal, Ralph 'forgot his wounds' and 'became fear'.

Ralph is rescued just in time by the arrival of the naval officer. The <u>images</u> <u>of</u> <u>war</u> – 'revolver', 'submachine gun' and 'cruiser' –

Text commentary

Explore

What has Ralph learned by this point in the novel? Compare the boy who turned a cartwheel on the beach in Chapter 1 with the creature on the beach now.

remind us that the boys left a war-torn society and will return to the remains of one. The presence of the officer restores a form of <u>civilised</u> <u>law</u> <u>and</u> <u>order</u>. He comes from the sea, and the conch, <u>symbol</u> of <u>democratic</u> <u>authority</u>, also came from the sea. But the boys thought that the beast came from the sea. What conclusions can you draw from this apparent contradiction?

The island society has produced <u>tyranny</u> and <u>chaos</u>, and the officer's reaction to Ralph is understandably one of 'wary astonishment'. How do you react to the almost magical appearance of the officer at this point in the novel?

Is this a straightforward 'happy ending'? In real life, do you think that 'the cavalry' always arrives just in time, as in films? Or is Golding making a point by ending the novel in this way, rather than in a believable (but unspeakably horrific) way?

Ralph speaks to the officer shyly, 'squirming a little, conscious of his filthy ... appearance'. In the light of the hunt, is this sudden switch of manner convincing? Or would you expect Ralph to react in this way?

Notice the devastating <u>irony</u> of 'Having a war or something?' The officer does not <u>understand</u> the situation. Who do you think knows more about the true nature of human beings – the adult or the dirty 'little boys' in front of him?

The naval officer is not presented as a character but as a <u>symbol</u> of the civilised, adult world. This raises the matter of the kind of world to which the boys will be taken. Notice the telling way he says 'We'll take you off', not that he'll take them 'home'. The officer sees Jack as 'a little boy', a 'little scarecrow' and a 'kid'. The effect of this is to scale everything down to size.

> **'Who's boss here?' 'I am',**
> **said Ralph loudly.**

From what you have learned about Ralph, why do you think he <u>claims</u> the <u>leadership</u> here? Our final view of Jack is of a <u>'little boy'</u>. Why do you think Jack decided not to claim the leadership? Piggy's glasses hang as a trophy at Jack's waist. They are a poignant reminder of him, and represent the tribe's loss of reason.

The officer tells them that they saw their smoke from the fire. Ironically the fire, which Ralph once saw as his only possibility of rescue, has at last brought it: but this fire was lit for quite another reason.

The officer's words about 'British boys' being 'able to put up a better show' echo the earlier, <u>civilised standards</u> of the boys. Can you hear the echo of Jack's words: 'After all … We're English' (Chapter 2)? Like the boys at the start of the book, the officer assumes that being civilised and reasonable come naturally. But notice how he also calls them a <u>'pack'</u>.

> **'Jolly good show.'**

The officer refers to a nineteenth-century novel, *Coral Island*. But that novel, though concerned with a group of stranded boys, is not a study in <u>realism</u> in the way *Lord of the Flies* is. The officer's comment illustrates his <u>ignorance</u> of what has really taken place on the island.

By the end of the novel, fire has destroyed the island. Golding implies that the atomic warfare mentioned in Chapter 1 may already have destroyed the rest of the earth. The boys are no more evil, <u>destructive or</u>

irresponsible than the adults have been. 'The burning wreckage of the island' illustrates the loss of paradise and the loss of innocence. The fire is an image of blazing hell, from which the children emerge completely changed.

Ralph wept for the end of innocence

Explore

Why is the officer embarrassed by the boys' tears? Why does Golding present a warship as the final image? What does this imply about the world the boys return to?

Has Golding ever actually shown the boys as 'innocent'? Seeing the novel as a fable, Ralph's tears could be caused by the recognition of the fallen nature of all humankind. Innocence can sometimes be confused with plain ignorance. Ralph can no longer see the world as secure, because he has gained knowledge of the evil which lurks in 'the darkness of man's heart'.

The darkness of man's heart.

'The darkness of man's heart' is a reference to *Heart of Darkness*, a short novel by Joseph Conrad, set in the African jungle and dealing with the force of evil, especially within people. What do you think is the 'darkness' which Golding believes is within the heart of all humankind? Now that you have read the novel, try to put an explanation of this 'darkness' into your own words.

Text commentary

Uncover the plot

Delete two of the three alternatives given, to find the correct plot.

1   Simon recovers from his fit and returns to the beach/destroys the Lord of the Flies/climbs the mountain to discover the truth about 'the beast'/the conch/the chief.

2   He sets out to tell the others. Ralph and Piggy break up/join/set fire to Jack's party; as a violent storm breaks, Percival/the littlun with the birthmark/Simon returns and is killed by the dancing, chanting Roger/beast/group.

3   The reign of the Lord of the Flies/Jack/Roger over his tribe becomes increasingly tyrannical/democratic/friendly.

4   After he burns/raids/breaks up Ralph's camp and steals Piggy's glasses/Sam 'n' Eric/the conch, the two/three/four boys go to Castle Rock and demand them back.

5   The twins defect/are killed/are captured, and Roger/Jack/Bill sends a great rock down which kills Piggy and smashes the conch. Ralph breaks down/gives up/escapes.

6   Sam 'n' Eric warn him that Jack intends to hunt him down. A desperate chase follows, during which Ralph/the savages/a naval officer set(s) fire to the island. The smoke attracts a British cruiser.

What? When? Why? How?

1   Why does Simon free the lines of the parachute from the rock? (Chapter 9)

2   How does Jack preside over his feast? (Chapter 9)

3   What happens to the dead parachutist? (Chapter 9)

4   What was Jack's original reason for raiding Ralph's camp? (Chapter 10)

5   What kind of fire has Jack's tribe lit? (Chapter 11)

6   When does Ralph finally lose his temper? (Chapter 11)

7   When does Ralph think Jack will 'let him alone'? (Chapter 12)

8   Why does Ralph weep? (Chapter 12)

Writing essays on *Lord of the Flies*

Exams

- To prepare for an exam, you should read the text through *at least twice*, preferably *three times*. In order to answer an exam question on it you need to know it very well.

- If you are studying the text for an 'open book' exam, make sure that you take your copy of the text with you. However, do not rely on it too much – you haven't got time. If you are not allowed to take the text in with you, you will need to memorise brief quotations.

- Read all the questions carefully before deciding which one you are going to answer. Choose the question that best allows you to demonstrate your understanding and personal ideas.

- Make sure that you understand exactly what the question is asking you to do.

- Plan your answer carefully before starting to write your essay (see page 70).

- Always begin your answer with a short introduction which gives an overview of the topic. Use your plan to help keep you focused on the question as you write the essay. Try to leave enough time to write a brief conclusion.

- Remember to use the **point–quotation–comment** approach, where you make a point, support it with a short quotation, then comment on it. Use short and relevant quotations – do not waste time copying out chunks of the text.

- Make sure that you know how much time you have for each question and stick to it.

- Leave enough time at the end of the exam to check your work through carefully and correct any spelling or other mistakes that you have made.

- Timing is not as crucial for coursework essays, so this is your chance to show what you can really do, without having to write under pressure. Do not leave your coursework essays until the last minute though. If you have to rush your work it is unlikely to be the best you can produce.

- Coursework allows you to go into more detail and develop your ideas in greater depth. The required length of assignments varies, and your teacher will advise you on this.

- If you have a choice of title, make sure you choose one which you are interested in and which gives you the chance to develop your ideas.

- Plan your essay carefully (see page 70). Refer to your plan and the essay title as you write, to check that you are staying on course.

- Use quotations in your essay, but beware of using them **too frequently** or making them **too long**. Often, the best quotes are just one or two words or short phrases. Make sure that they are relevant to the points that you are making.

- If your topic requires it, use appropriate background information and put the text in a cultural and historical context. Remember, though, that the text itself should be at the centre of your essay.

- Include a short conclusion which sums up the key points of your ideas.

- Do not copy any of your essay from another source, e.g. other notes or the Internet. This is called plagiarism, and it is very serious if the exam board find that you have done this.

- If you have used sources, list them in a bibliography at the end of the essay.

- If you are allowed to word process your essay, it will be easier to make changes and to re-draft it.

Key quotations

&& This toy of voting was almost as pleasing as the conch. &&

This quotation is taken from Chapter 1. It can be used to illustrate how the boys begin by democratically electing a leader. The idea of 'toy', though, suggests that they may soon tire of this idea and that things will change.

&& Ralph made a step forward and Jack smacked Piggy's head. Piggy's glasses flew off and tinkled on the rocks. &&

This quotation is taken from Chapter 4, where Jack and his hunters have let the fire go out as a ship passed the island. It can be used to illustrate the first real confrontation between Jack and Ralph, and also the first signs of violence breaking out as Jack hits Piggy. It also shows how Piggy becomes the focus of Jack's anger and violence.

&& Kill the pig! Cut his throat! Kill the pig! Bash him in! &&

This quotation is taken from Chapter 7 and is the chant taken up by the hunters as they play a ritual 'game' of hunting Robert. It can be used to illustrate the kind of group hysteria that takes over the children and foreshadows the point later in the novel where a similar 'hunt' ends in the killing of Simon.

> ❝Simon was crying out something about a dead man on a hill. 'Kill the beast! Cut his throat! Spill his blood! Do him in!'❞

This quotation is taken from Chapter 9 and is the point at which Simon is killed by the hunters. It can be used to illustrate the first deliberate killing and the way in which the hunters' frenzy causes them to lose all sense of 'civilised' behaviour.

> ❝The rock struck Piggy a glancing blow from chin to knee; the conch exploded into a thousand white fragments and ceased to exist.❞

This quotation is taken from Chapter 11 and describes the moment at which Piggy is killed and the conch destroyed. It can be used to show the quite deliberate murder of Piggy by Roger, and the fact that he is killed at the same time that the conch, the symbol of order and civilised behaviour, is destroyed.

> ❝Ralph wept for the end of innocence, the darkness of man's heart, and the fall though the air of the true, wise friend called Piggy.❞

This quotation is taken from Chapter 12, at the end of the novel. It comes as Ralph is rescued from certain death by the arrival of the naval officer. It can be used to illustrate how Ralph has lost his childhood innocence through his ordeal on the island and now understands the brutality and cruelty that human beings are capable of.

1. *What do you think* Lord of the Flies *has to say about human nature?*

2. *Explore the roles and importance of Simon and Roger in* Lord of the Flies.

3. *What is the significance of the 'Beast' in the novel? How does Golding use this idea to explore the nature of fear?*

4. *Read again the passage from near the end of Chapter 2,* Fire on the Mountain, *starting 'Beneath the capering boys a quarter of a mile…' to 'Piggy glanced nervously into hell and cradled the conch.'*

5. *Do you think that the island was hell for the boys? You should refer to the experiences of at least two boys in your answer.*

6. *What do you learn about leadership in this novel? You may wish to consider:*
   - *Ralph's election as leader*
   - *some of Piggy's ideas*
   - *Jack's cruelty to others*
   - *the hunt for Ralph at the end.*

7. *How far do you agree that the breaking up of the boys into the two opposing groups was inevitable? You should refer closely to events and characters in your answer.*

8. *Look again at the first three pages of Chapter 12,* Cry of the Hunters. *How much do you think that Ralph, at this point, has changed since the beginning of the novel? You should refer in detail to events, actions and language used.*

   What view of 'civilisation' does Golding present in Lord of the Flies?

9 How does what happens to Piggy on the island reflect the boys' descent from civilised standards into savagery? In your answer you should consider:
- Piggy's relationship with Ralph
- Jack's treament of Piggy
- Piggy's attitude towards the conch
- Piggy's death.

10 Explore Golding's presentation of the character of Jack in Lord of the Flies.

11 What is the importance of the conch in Lord of the Flies? In your answer you should consider:
- what the conch symbolises
- how the boys use it
- its destruction.

12 How important are rules and order in Lord of the Flies?

13 Compare the ways in which Ralph and Jack change during the course of Lord of the Flies.

14 In what ways is hunting important in Lord of the Flies?

15 Why is fire important in Lord of the Flies?

In order to write an effective essay, you need to approach your task in an organised way. You need to **plan** your essay carefully before beginning to write. This will help you to achieve a higher grade.

- The first thing to do is read the question carefully to make sure that you fully understand it, then highlight key words.

- You will need to make notes on the topic in order to start preparing your ideas. You can do this in various ways, such as making a list of key points, or creating a spidergram or a mind map.

- One advantage of using mind maps or spidergrams is that they help you to create links between the various points you make. Put the title of the essay in the middle of a page and add your points around it. You can then draw lines to connect up various points or ideas, linking them in a clear, visual way.

- If you wish, you can colour code your ideas, or even add pictures or symbols if that helps you to think about your ideas more clearly.

- Since mind maps and spidergrams are a way of charting your knowledge, they are also an excellent revision aid. You could work through a number of essay titles in this way. (See some examples of spidergrams on the following pages.)

- In the planning stage of your essay it is also a good idea to jot down some useful quotations. These should be kept brief and to the point, and can be added to your spidergram.

- It can also be useful to plan what you are going to write in each paragraph of your essay. You can number the branches on your spidergram, so that you are clear about the order of your points. This will help you to structure your work more effectively.

- Remember that you are much more likely to write an effective essay if you do some planning before you start to write it.

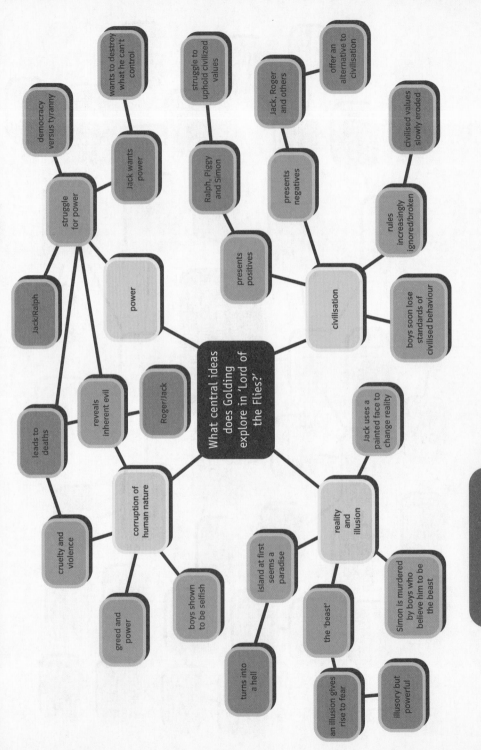

Central node: What central ideas does Golding explore in 'Lord of the Flies?'

power
- struggle for power
  - democracy versus tyranny
  - Jack wants power
    - wants to destroy what he can't control
  - Jack/Ralph
  - leads to deaths
    - cruelty and violence

civilisation
- presents positives
  - Ralph, Piggy and Simon
    - struggle to uphold civilized values
- presents negatives
  - Jack, Roger and others
    - offer an alternative to civilisation
- civilised values slowly eroded
- rules increasingly ignored/broken
- boys soon lose standards of civilised behaviour

corruption of human nature
- reveals inherent evil
  - Roger/Jack
- greed and power
- boys shown to be selfish

reality and illusion
- Jack uses a painted face to change reality
- Simon is murdered by boys who believe him to be the beast
- Island at first seems a paradise
  - turns into a hell
- the 'beast'
  - an illusion gives rise to fear
  - illusory but powerful

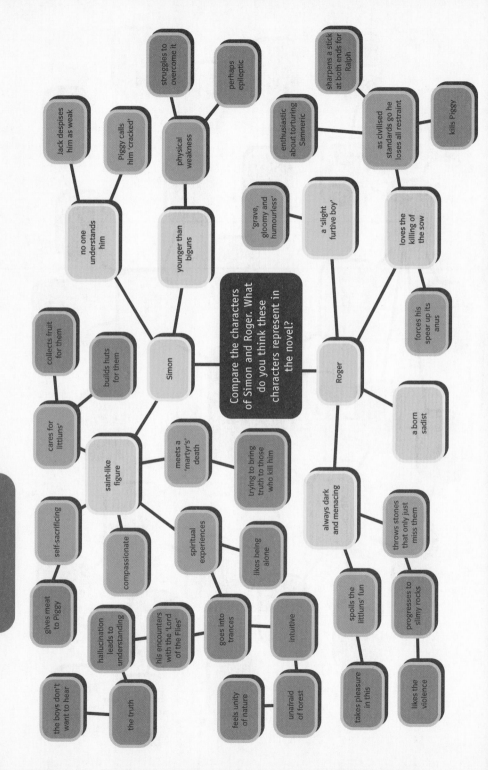

Compare the characters of Simon and Roger. What do you think these characters represent in the novel?

Simon

- no one understands him
  - Jack despises him as weak
  - Piggy calls him 'cracked'
- younger than biguns
- physical weakness
  - struggles to overcome it
  - perhaps epileptic
- collects fruit for them
- builds huts for them
- cares for littluns'
- saint-like figure
  - self-sacrificing
    - gives meat to Piggy
  - compassionate
  - meets a 'martyr's' death
    - trying to bring truth to those who kill him
- spiritual experiences
  - likes being alone
  - goes into trances
  - intuitive
    - feels unity of nature
    - unafraid of forest
  - his encounters with the 'Lord of the Flies'
    - hallucination leads to understanding
- the truth
  - the boys don't want to hear

Roger

- 'grave, gloomy and humourless'
- a 'slight furtive boy'
- loves the killing of the sow
  - forces his spear up its anus
- enthusiastic about torturing Samneric
- as civilised standards go he loses all restraint
  - sharpens a stick at both ends for Ralph
  - kills Piggy
- a born sadist
- always dark and menacing
  - throws stones that only just miss them
    - progresses to slimy rocks
    - likes the violence
  - spoils the littluns' fun
    - takes pleasure in this

72

Examine Golding's presentation of the character of Piggy and his contribution to the novel.

Central topic: Examine Golding's presentation of the character of Piggy and his contribution to the novel.

most intelligent of the boys
- acquires an adult way of thinking
  - adult
  - illness has given him time to think
- serious respect for adult values
  - recognises in him basic decency

loyal to Ralph
- tries to influence and manipulate Ralph
  - knows that Ralph is the only one who can stand up to Jack

recognises the value of the conch
- symbol of democracy
  - conch and Piggy destroyed together
- tries to protect it
  - fragile-like the values it represents

hatred inflicted on Piggy
- becomes half-blind
- almost entirely blind
- corresponds with stages of boys descent into savagery

working-class background
- working-class in speech

fatherless

Piggy known only by his nickname

an 'outsider' figure
- timid
- his poor eyesight
- his asthma
- recognises himself as an outsider
- his laziness
- his fortress
- boys enjoy jokes at his expense

Sample response

Compare the characters of Jack and Ralph in *Lord of the Flies*

Ralph is twelve years old and is a fair-haired, athletic boy. ✓ Golding describes him very favourably and makes him seem a leader-type figure. ✓ Right from the start of the novel he comes across as a leader figure and it is he who blows the conch at the beginning of the story and this gets all the other boys to come out to him. ✓

He is shown as a fair-minded kind of boy ✓ and he is quite nice to Piggy, who is the most intelligent of all the boys, and because he is nice to him Piggy helps him by giving him advice. Piggy is fat and not fit and is the type that gets picked on a lot and so he wants Ralph to stand up for him and protect him. Really Ralph is the only one who can stop Jack having a go at Piggy and even Ralph has trouble with Jack. ✓

When everyone else arrives Ralph is voted leader, although it is obvious that Jack doesn't like this idea and is really put out about it. ✓ Jack has a funny kind of respect for Ralph here though, and so he doesn't kick up a fuss and goes along with it. Ralph shows he thinks about Jack's feelings, though, by making him in charge of hunting. ✓

Jack, on the other hand, is much keener to be leader than Ralph and is pretty put out when he is not voted in. ✓ Although he accepts that Ralph is leader to begin with, he turns against him later and takes over the leadership himself by force and by scaring everyone to follow him. ✓

It is obvious from the start that Jack is used to being in charge when he arrives with the choir and he tells them what to do in a really bossy way: 'Choir! Stand still'. The description of him also gives you a picture of a boy who could be nasty: 'he was tall, thin and bony' and 'his face was crumpled' and his eyes were 'ready to turn to anger'. ✓

Unlike Ralph, Jack makes people do what he wants them to do out of fear. ✓ Eventually he challenges Ralph to be leader and the two fight. Although neither really wins this fight, Jack is able to take over as leader because the others are too frightened to do anything. He gradually gets more and more vicious and nasty, and Simon and Piggy are killed and Ralph only escapes because the grown-ups arrive to rescue them all. ✓

Overall Ralph tries to stick to civilised-type behaviour but Jack turns into a savage. This can be seen by how he and his 'tribe' paint their faces and act like savages. ✓

Examiner's comments

This response shows a good focus on the question and makes a range of relevant points about Ralph and Jack. There is a clear understanding of the difference between the two and textual references are used to support the ideas. There is good understanding shown of the presentation of both characters and clear knowledge of the text. The response is clearly expressed and accurately written although some colloquial phrases are used.